P9-ARC-603

THE LONG CHALKBOARD

THE LONG CHALKBOARD

— *and Other Stories* —

Jenny Allen
Illustrated by Jules Feiffer

PANTHEON BOOKS, NEW YORK

Copyright © 2006 by Jenny Allen
Illustrations copyright © 2006 by Jules Feiffer

All rights reserved. Published in the United States by Pantheon Books,
a division of Random House, Inc., New York,
and in Canada by Random House of Canada Limited, Toronto.

Pantheon Books and colophon are registered trademarks of Random House, Inc.

Library of Congress Cataloging-in-Publication Data
Allen, Jenny.
    The long chalkboard, and other stories / by Jenny Allen; illustrated by
Jules Feiffer.
        p.   cm.
    ISBN 0-375-42453-9
    1. Fables, American. I. Feiffer, Jules. II. Title.
    PS3601.L42L66   2006
    813'.6—dc22
                                                        2006043187

www.pantheonbooks.com
Printed in Singapore
First Edition
2 4 6 8 9 7 5 3 1

For Kate, Halley, and Julie

THE LONG CHALKBOARD

Once there was a girl named Caroline.
All she wanted was a husband and three children.

When she grew up, she got them all.

Her apartment was so big, there was room for a playroom in it.
When they moved in, Caroline had an idea: she covered
one entire wall of the playroom with a chalkboard.

"Here is some chalk," she told her children. "Write whatever you like."

wrote one.   wrote another.   wrote the third.

Caroline wept. "They're not creative," she told her husband.
"So what," he said. "You're not creative, I'm not creative."

Caroline went to bed for two days.

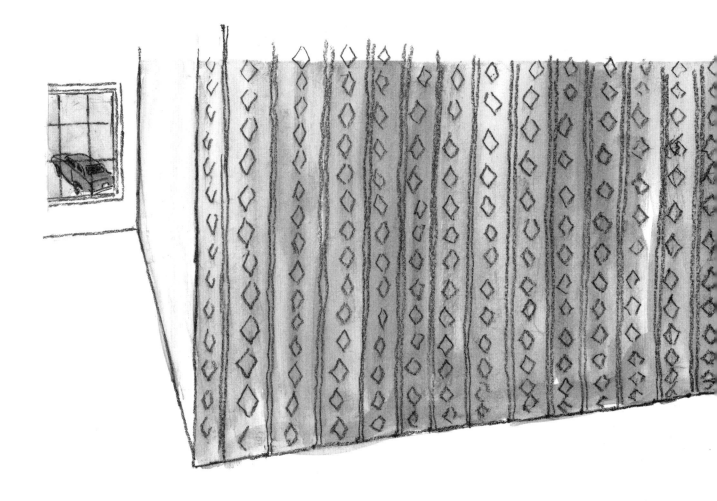

Then she wallpapered over the chalkboard. A year later, they moved to Montclair, New Jersey.

The family that moved into the apartment had a mother, a father, and a boy.
The boy loved only one thing, which was math.

In steaming off the wallpaper, which they hated, the parents discovered the chalkboard. "We're getting rid of it, of course," they said. "Please don't," the boy begged. "I need it." "All right already," said the parents, who thought he was strange.

Every day the boy wrote out math problems on the chalkboard and solved them. One day he invented his own math problem, a problem never seen before. His teachers came to see it,

and their teachers, and their teachers' teachers, and the presidents of the country's three most prestigious universities, and the editor of a famous magazine.

He was the youngest student ever admitted to the country's three most prestigious universities.
He picked the one farthest from home,

where he met a girl who also loved math.

Four years later, they were married at their favorite campus spot, the Slice of π Café.

But his parents didn't like the girl, so he never visited them.

If he had, he would have seen that they had painted over the chalkboard, in celadon green, and turned the room into a media center.

After they retired and moved to Boca Raton,

another family moved in.
Underneath a layer of celadon, a housepainter found the chalkboard.

"Leave it!" said the daughter, who wanted to direct movies
when she grew up and who was already good at giving directions.

“Of course, sweetie,” said her parents.

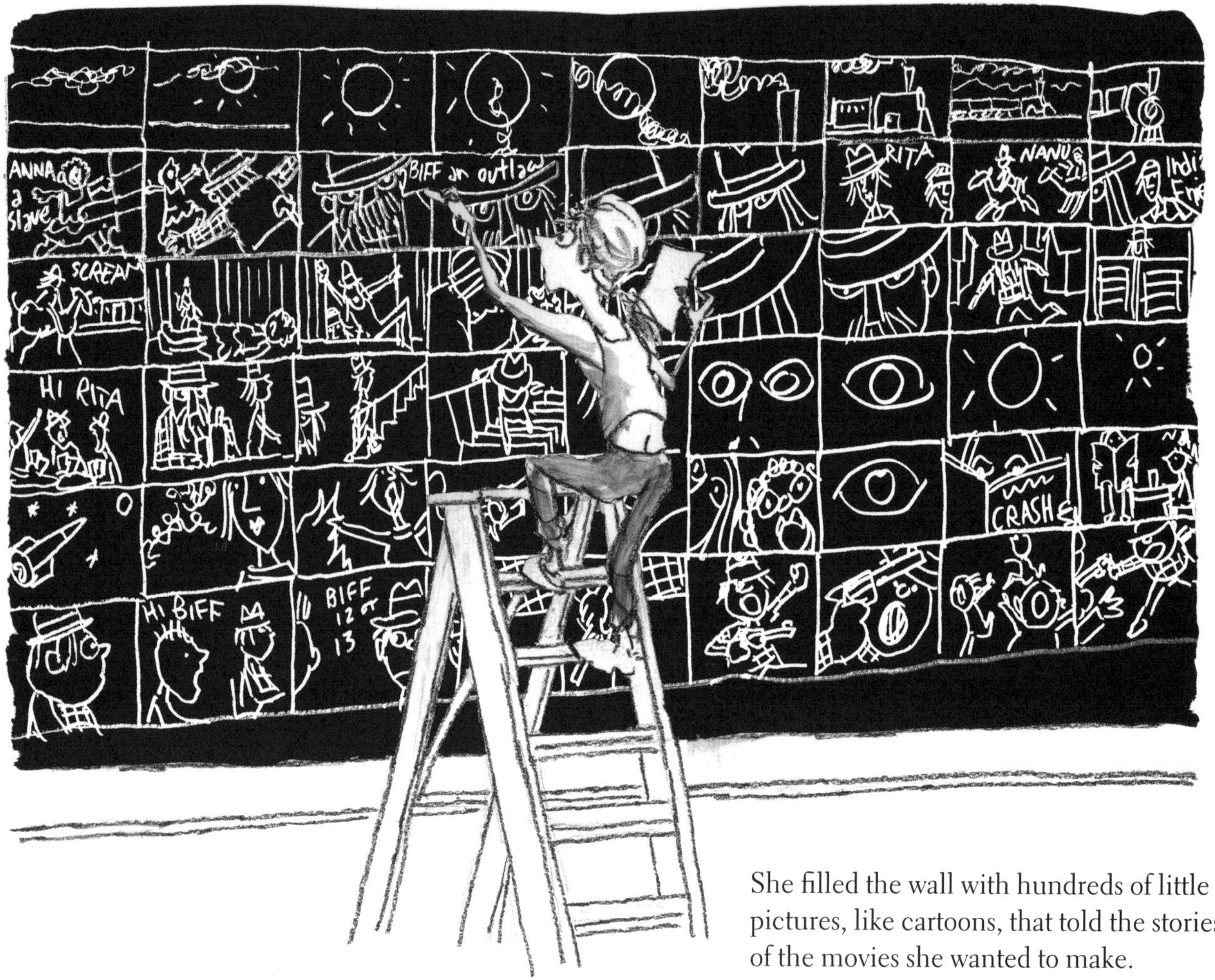
ANNA a slave
BIFF an outlaw
RITA
NANU
SCREAM
HI RITA
CRASH
HI BIFF
BIFF 12 or 13

She filled the wall with hundreds of little pictures, like cartoons, that told the stories of the movies she wanted to make.

Instead of going to college, she turned one of her cartoons into a movie. It was a brilliant movie, with adventure and heartbreak and, just when things seemed most tragic, a happy ending.

Critics loved it. Audiences loved it. It won every award a movie could win. It was an instant classic.

The girl moved to Hollywood and made more movies.

The girl's parents kept the cartoons on the chalkboard, polyurethaning them to preserve them.

Visitors to the apartment enjoyed looking at the drawings.

One visitor, the friend of a friend, was the president of a famous museum in Washington, D.C. "This chalkboard represents an important piece of our nation's cultural history," he said.

The girl's parents agreed and donated the chalkboard
to the museum, where it was put on permanent display.
Young filmmakers came from all over the world to see it.

So did the girl, whose subsequent films, although successful, lacked the je ne sais quoi of her first work.

Time and again, she sat for hours in front of the drawings, trying to recapture whatever it was she had lost.

"Take it down," she told the museum president one day. "Put it away."
She was still good at giving directions, so he did what she told him to do.

The chalkboard was stored in the vast basement of the museum, alongside the living room furniture from a beloved television program, a collection of hula hoops, and a Tiffany window.

One day, the museum president told his staff that drastic budget cuts from the government meant that the museum had no choice but to immediately sell some of its possessions.

At an auction at a famous auction house, the museum sold off many pieces from its collection, including the chalkboard.

The chalkboard fetched an
extraordinary sum—

in part because an enterprising
young financial officer at the
auction house had the idea
of slicing the chalkboard into
many sections and selling
them separately.

The section that sold for the highest sum showed the film's well-earned happy ending,

and was bought by an old woman in a stylish hat who had been seen visiting the chalkboards every day for a week before the auction.

She would stand in front of the piece, looking at it; sometimes she smiled.

When a reporter from the newspaper asked her why she had bought it, she told him that she had always loved the movie.

"My husband is dead, and I don't understand my children," she said. "I feel less lonely when I look at it."

She took the piece home to Montclair, New Jersey,

where she mounted it across from the chair
she sat in while she sipped her nightly glass of sherry.

And every day until she died, the happy ending gave Caroline more pleasure than she had felt since before she could remember.

WHAT HAPPENED

Audrey wrote books for children. They were called the "What Happened to . . ." books. *What Happened to Christie's Christmas Tree?* was one; *What Happened to Paul's Purim Costume?* and *What Happened to Dolma's Saga Dawa Dumplings?* were some others.

Children loved the books because they were whodunits. Grown-ups loved them because they were educational and had uplift. In the process of looking for the object that something had happened to, the children in the books always discovered the True Meaning of important holidays and Valuable Lessons about themselves. Audrey had won several commendations from the Librarians' League and had twice been a finalist for a coveted Kenny Award, bestowed by the Juvenile Booksellers' Association and named for the child of the JBA's husband-and-wife founders.

One day, passing by her neighborhood bookstore, Audrey noticed a poster in the window. The poster showed the cover of a book: *David Makes a Dreidel.* Underneath the cover, the poster read, "Book Signing with Author/Illustrator Simon Shayne Tonight."

In the children's section, Audrey found *David Makes a Dreidel* featured in a display of holiday books, which, she could not help noticing, included none by her.

David Makes a Dreidel was not a whodunit, but the child in the story discovered a Valuable Lesson about himself and about the True Meaning of an important holiday. Worse, the jacket on the book urged readers to watch for the author's next volume,
Caitlin Makes a Christmas Wreath.

Furious, Audrey went to see her editor.

"Some creep named Simon Shayne has stolen my idea," said Audrey.

"That may be so," said her editor, "but I'm afraid there isn't anything we can do about it." Her editor had seen *David Makes a Dreidel* but hadn't found the right time to mention it to Audrey, who tended to be thin-skinned. She explained that Audrey did not own the idea of writing books about children and holidays, and that the best Audrey could do would be to think of Simon Shayne's books as a kind of compliment to her.

"Oh, please," said Audrey. For a moment, she considered finding another publishing company; then she remembered that her editor had believed in the first "What Happened to . . ." book when every other publishing company had turned it down.

"Couldn't you at least write
him a mean letter?" said Audrey.
     "Bad business, sweetie," said her editor. "I'm sorry.
I really am. Why don't you go get yourself a manicure and forget all about it?"

Audrey, who had never gotten herself a manicure and did not know how to forget about anything, instead returned to the bookstore, in time for the signing.

Simon Shayne sat behind a table, signing books for a long line of parents and children. As he signed, he chatted with the customers, often throwing his head back to laugh a big and, to Audrey's mind, show-offy laugh. The line moved at a snail's pace, and no wonder: Audrey overheard him say to each customer who approached, "Now whom shall I say this is for?"

Audrey had a policy against personalizing books at signings, having found it time-consuming and irritating. First, the customer had to spell his or her name,

or the name of the niece or grandchild the book was for. This exchange, Audrey had noticed, seemed to make the customer feel that he or she was now on familiar terms with Audrey, who then had to answer questions or look at baby pictures or relate for the umpteenth time where she got her ideas (she was particularly uncomfortable with this subject, since her books were basically one idea repeated, however cleverly, over and over). She found that signing her name with, at most, a simple "Happy Holidays" worked best.

Finally, it was Audrey's turn in front of the desk. "And whom shall I say this is for?" Simon Shayne asked her, smiling and reaching for a book from the stack beside him.

"I'm not buying a book," Audrey said. "I'm the author of the 'What Happened to . . .' series."
"Come again?" said Simon Shayne, looking confused.

"Don't 'Come again' me," said Audrey. "I'm the one you stole your idea from." She pulled from her tote bag the copies of *What Happened to Christie's Christmas Tree?* and *What Happened to Danny's Dreidel?* that she had brought for just this moment.

Simon Shayne looked at both books carefully, inside and out.

"I can see why you're upset," he said not unkindly, looking her in the eye, "but I've never heard of your books."

It was true: Simon Shayne was a high school art teacher who enjoyed making things and had written his books, complete with step-by-step instructions, to encourage children to do the same.

Audrey wanted to say, "I find that hard to believe," but she couldn't. She believed him.

"Be that as it may," she said, "you have to stop writing your books."

"I can't do that," said Simon Shayne.

Steaming, Audrey strode down the street to her favorite coffee shop, where she tried to console herself with a cup of split-pea soup and the newspaper.

In the section on the upcoming weekend's cultural events, she noticed a headline: "Fun Stuff for Kids." She disliked the word "stuff," which she considered lazy and slangy, and was contemplating writing a letter to the editor to complain, when her eye caught a listing for a reading at her local branch of the public library: "Neighborhood author/illustrator Simon Shayne will read from his new book, *David Makes a Dreidel.*" There would also be a surprise activity for which children were told to "B.Y.O.S.—Bring Your Own Soap."

Simon Shayne lived in her neighborhood? Why didn't he just take over her lease and start wearing her clothes?

On Saturday morning, Audrey went to the library. Her plan was to peek into the children's room, see what kind of crowd Simon Shayne had drawn, and leave.

The children's room was packed with children and their parents. Apparently, Simon Shayne had finished reading; his audience sat at tables, busily working at their activity.

Using plastic butter knives, they were carving dreidels out of bars of soap while Simon Shayne walked among them, offering encouraging words. Suddenly, Audrey saw Simon Shayne looking at her.

"Well, hello!" he called, before she could make a getaway. "Kids, I'd like you to meet the author of the 'What Happened to . . .' books, Ms.—"

"Audrey Lasker!" the children's librarian, who recognized Audrey from her book-jacket photographs, piped up just in time.

The roomful of parents and children, most of whom had at least one of Audrey's books at home, beamed at her.

"Come in and join us!" said Simon Shayne. "I didn't bring any soap," said Audrey. "I brought extra!" said Simon Shayne. Of course he had.

"I'll get you started," he said, taking Audrey by the elbow.

He cleared a place for her at one of the tables and showed her how to whittle the soap. Before returning to help the others, he wished her good luck with her dreidel and gave her a wink, as if they were in on some good-natured joke together.

Audrey never made things, not even her own breakfast,
considering herself hopeless at any endeavor that required using her hands.
She dearly wished not to be here but saw no escape: the parents and children at her table
were all smiling at her, mistaking her for a children's book author like Simon Shayne, the cheerful,
child-at-heart kind, the kind who would come to the library on a Saturday morning to gamely join in
the fun. It always rankled her when, because of her profession, others assumed she was better-natured
than she was, but she had never actually felt trapped by the misunderstanding before.

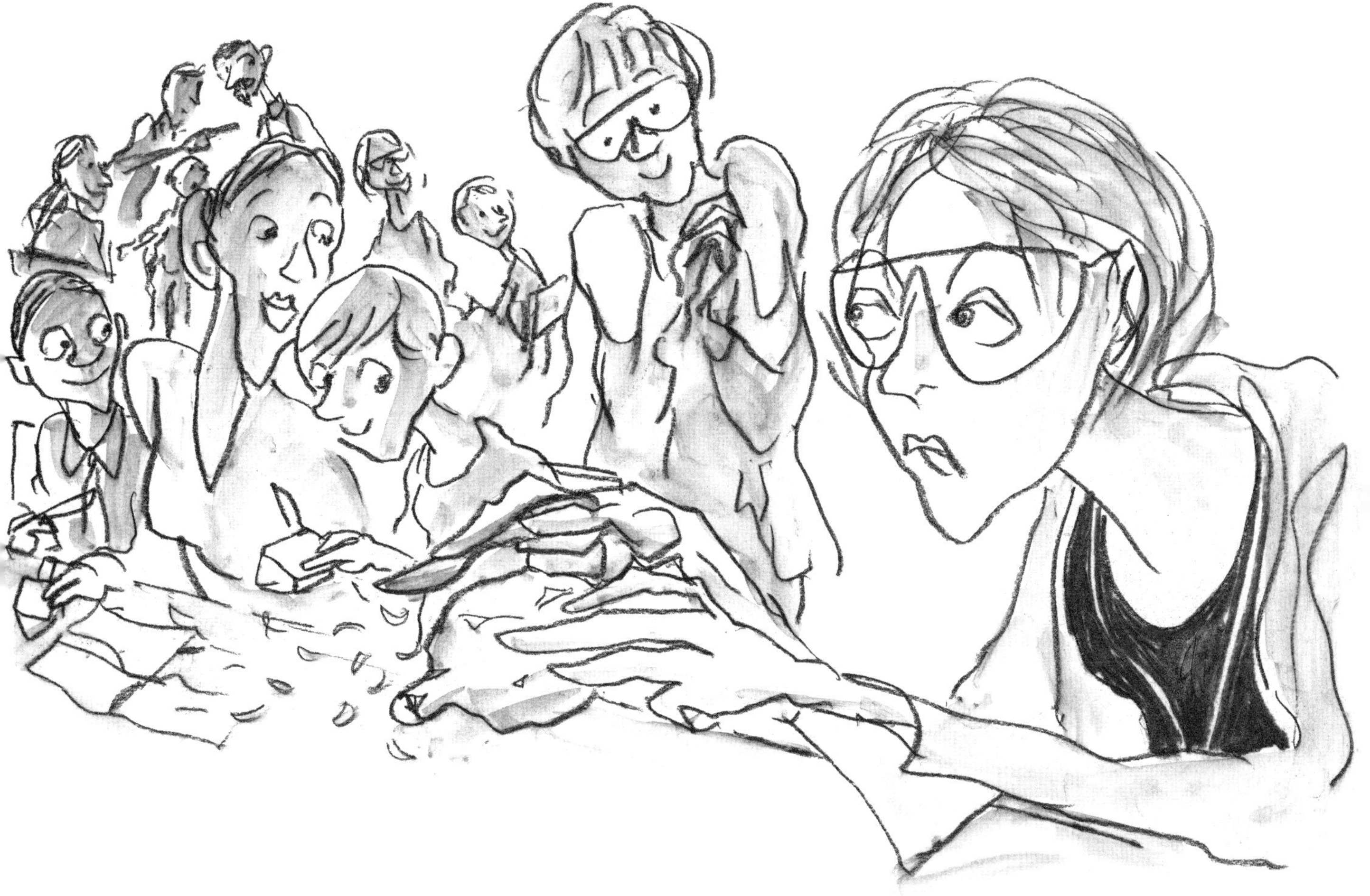

In spite of her self-consciousness, however, Audrey found that she liked working at her little project: shaving curly slices of soap off the bar, watching it change shape, tapering the tip to a fine point. She was absorbed in her work, so much so that she felt vaguely sad when she realized that she had, in fact, finished. She had made a dreidel.

Parents and children were leaving; the morning's program, it seemed, was over. Audrey, surprised at herself for having stayed so long, quickly pulled on her coat.

"Good job!" said Simon Shayne, who had appeared at her side and now pointed to the dreidel on the table in front of her.

"I'm so glad you two got to meet," said the children's librarian, who stood next to him. "Your books remind me so much of each other's."

"No kidding," said Audrey,
snatching up her dreidel and leaving the library.

Two days later, Audrey received a letter in the mail:

Simon Shayne

Dear Ms. Lasker,

Thank you for coming to the event at the library.
I sense that you are still agitated about the similarity
of our books, and I have an idea to discuss with you.
I'd like to meet this Thursday at The Spotted Zebra.
You needn't decide on coming until the last minute—
I'll be there regardless, at 5 p.m.

Sincerely,

Simon Shayne

Audrey felt that it would be churlish not to go, particularly, she had to admit, when he was making it so easy for her not to. On Thursday she arrived at The Spotted Zebra, a local café that catered to Anglophiles. She saw him first, sitting in a corner in front of tea for two—scones and crustless sandwiches and a pot of tea.

Spotting her, Simon Shayne smiled and waved widely—the way a person does who is actually looking forward to seeing another person, Audrey noted, feeling confused.

"I'm glad you came," said Simon Shayne.

"You're welcome," said Audrey.

"Okay," said Simon Shayne. "Here's what I propose.

We'll split the holidays—you take some; I'll take others. That way we'll never do the same ones."

"All right," said Audrey, glancing at the scones, the clotted cream, the little British flags sticking out of bud vases on the tables. "You can have St. Swithin's Day. I'll take Easter."

A flicker of hurt showed in Simon Shayne's eyes.

"I'm sorry," said Audrey, "but I'm not divvying up the world's holidays with you. What if I happen to get a great idea for one of your holidays? What if I can't think of anything for one of mine?"

"But we could—"

"Look," she said, "not everyone plays well with others. That's why people become writers."

"Some people," he said.

This time it was Simon Shayne who left abruptly, though not without leaving enough money to cover the tea and a tip.

A few days later, Audrey sat at her desk, writing her new book, *What Happened to Otaro's Oshogatsu Origami?* (Origami, she had learned, was not associated with any particular Japanese holiday, but Audrey liked the idea and gave herself poetic license.) As a rule, Audrey's characters didn't make the objects that mysteriously disappeared, but it seemed logical
for Otaro to make his own.

And if he was going to make his own, she had
better try making some herself, so that she could describe
the process. She thought, remembering her dreidel experience,
maybe it would be fun. The crane, she learned on the Web, was a popular origami figure.

She bought a book of origami instructions and some brightly colored origami paper at the art-supply store and took them to her coffee shop, settling in at a booth by the window. Between sips of split-pea soup, Audrey tried to make a crane.

She followed the directions, folding the square of paper this way and that, unfolding it and starting all over again, but nothing crane-shaped came of her efforts.

Far from it: the little worked-over square looked like a wad of used Kleenex, nothing more. She tried again, with a fresh square, and again. A half-dozen crumpled pieces of paper lay on the table in front of her.

Suddenly, the pieces of paper lost their edges, their colors blurring together. When Audrey blinked, she realized that she was crying. She was crying, and she could not stop.

Someone was speaking to her.

"I was just passing by," the voice said. It was Simon Shayne. "And I noticed that you might need a little help." He sat down next to her.

He took one of the clumped-up pieces of paper, smoothed it out, and, consulting the directions, slowly folded it into the shape of a crane.

He did the same thing with another piece, and another, until he had made cranes out of every square except one. This square he placed in front of Audrey.

Together, with his hands guiding hers,
they made the last crane.

* * *

There were few surprises at that year's Kenny Awards luncheon.

As usual, attendees complained about the annual appearance of chicken marsala on the menu. As usual, Kenny himself flew in from Scottsdale, Arizona—where, at forty-three years old, he still lived with his parents—to bibulously hand out the prizes.

One unexpected winner was Audrey Lasker, considered by many to be a perpetual runner-up. The award for best illustrated book went to *What Happened to Otaro's Oshogatsu Origami?*.

The judges agreed that the addition of lovely step-by-step instructions by her new illustrator enhanced the author's themes considerably.

Neither Audrey nor her collaborator was able to attend the ceremony. In accepting the award on their behalf, Audrey's editor explained that she and Simon Shayne were on an extended honeymoon,

discovering the True Meaning of this important holiday.

JUDY'S WONDER CHILI

Judy had a way with chili.

People who didn't usually like chili loved hers so much that it made them question what they had had against chili in the first place.

Chili aficionados loved hers the best of all chilis, and felt they had been promiscuous in their previous praise of this chili or that.

Judy made her chili for people she knew who had just had a baby, or lost someone they loved, or gotten bad news, or gotten sick.

Judy's chili did wonders. Exhausted parents felt fortified, ready to pace another five hours with a colicky newborn or deal with ailments, like projectile vomiting, that they had never heard of a week earlier and that they almost felt might have dissuaded them from having a baby at all, had someone clued them in.

People who had lost a loved one knew,
for the first time, that the day would
come when they would actually want
to get out of bed in the morning.

People who were sick felt better.
People who were very sick believed,
even when it was against the odds,
that they would get well.

"Judy," her friends told her,
"you really have to go into business."

Judy just laughed.

Even if she had any interest in going into business, which she didn't, she had no idea from one batch to the next how much of each ingredient she used, or even exactly which ingredients she used. Half the time she forgot to buy several important components and ended up using things she found in her cupboard.

"That was the best batch ever," friends would say. "What did you do?"

"Oh, I couldn't find any of something, so I had to use something else, but I forget what it was," she would say.

Some people thought she was being coy, but she was not. Judy was not that interested in chili per se; she was interested in giving it to people.

As a result, she didn't think about the chili
so much while she made it. She thought
about whatever book she was reading—which
she sometimes read while making the chili—
about whether her favorite baseball team was
going to get to the playoffs, and, of course, about
the people she was making the chili for.

Her musings tended to distract her. More than once
she had poured cornflakes into the simmering pot instead
of into her breakfast bowl, failing to notice as she stirred them in.

"Judy, did you put cornflakes in that chili you brought over last night?" her friends said to her. "Something in there looked sort of cornflakey."

"Oh, dear," she said. "I'm sorry."

"Don't be sorry, honey—it was incredible. Well, you're a riot, that's what you are."

"What did you put in it this time?" her friend Elaine said after hearing about one of the cornflake batches. "Your sock?"

"I hope not," Judy said, checking her feet.

"That's my Judy," said Elaine. Elaine was Judy's oldest friend. Elaine adored Judy but tended to condescend to her, even though Judy's chili had seen Elaine through a two-year postpartum depression, her husband's affairs with her son's first- and fourth-grade teachers, her son's conversion to Scientology, and, lately, a troublesome rotator cuff.

Judy did not remind Elaine or her other friends that the reason they were feeling well enough to tease Judy was because of the chili she had made for them. Like many people with a touch of eccentricity, she was often pigeonholed as cute, as a character. This tendency bothered her—but she didn't say anything about it.

Nor was she proprietary about her chili. Anyone who asked was welcomed into her kitchen to watch her make it. They wrote down in precise quantities every item she put into the pot and went home and put in the exact same things in the exact same order.

Judy's chili was nuanced and piquant. Theirs, too, was nuanced and piquant.

But not nuanced and piquant enough. Not enough to begin the mending of a broken heart, or soothe the sting of regret, or ease a bout of bursitis.

Not a few people who watched Judy make chili and then attempted to make it themselves were convinced that she had added something while they answered their cell phones.

Others, like Elaine, knew there was no explaining it. "It is what it is," said Elaine, who was fond of the expression.

One young couple in her building, husband-
and-wife entrepreneurs, had tried to market
Judy's chili. Judy had been riding on the
elevator with them one day when the wife
swooned and fell to the floor. They had just
gotten the news, the husband stammered,
that the wife would be having triplets and
that their long-delayed Guatemalan
adoption was finally going through.

Judy made the couple chili to help them through the shock, and
they felt so buoyed by it that they hatched the idea of
selling Judy's chili. They took a sample to
a lab, had its ingredients analyzed,
and sold it in cans labeled
"Well Be-an Chili—
Cures What Ails You."

It didn't cure what ailed anyone. The wife blamed her husband's bad faith—it was his idea not to let Judy in on their plan—for somehow hexing the chili. Soon, neither of them could bear to look at Judy in the elevator. After a year, they and their four toddlers and their three nannies moved to the suburbs, where the couple eventually divorced, done in by their secret guilt.

One day Judy made chili for another couple, dear friends who were going through a bad patch (scratched cornea, termites).

    That evening their son came for dinner.
Entranced with power since his sandbox days, the boy had grown up to become one of the governor's closest advisers. As usual, he spent the evening confusing his parents with long stories about arcane state politics. For perhaps the first time in his life, however, he also noticed the food he was eating.
    "This is fantastic," he said. "I've got to take some to Richard. Richard loves chili."

Richard was the governor, and Richard did indeed love chili—next to getting reelected, eating was his favorite thing to do, and chili was one of his favorite foods. Reluctantly, the adviser's parents turned over the extra chili Judy had given them for their freezer.

"But I want the Tupperware back," his mother told him. "That's Judy's container, and they don't make that model anymore."

The next morning, the adviser brought the chili to the governor, who devoured all of it, cold, right out of the container and in spite of reproving looks from his wife, who had stopped in on her way to coffee with the spouses of the members of the Peat Moss Packers' Association.

"Oh, my God, this is incredible," said the governor.

"Richard, at least close your mouth when you chew," said his wife.

Just then the governor got an idea. He asked the adviser to get Judy's number, then dialed it.

"This is the governor, but please call me Richard," said the governor after Judy had answered. "I want you to make a big batch of your amazing chili so I can serve it up to some friends of mine," he said, and then, more to himself than to Judy, "One hit of this stuff, and they'll throw money at me."

"Excuse me?" asked Judy.

"My reelection committee—I want to fire them up for the campaign with your chili. Get 'em excited."

"I'm sorry, but I can't help you," said Judy.

"Why not?" asked the governor.

"Because chili shouldn't have an agenda, Richard," said Judy.

Even with the adviser cajoling on the extension, Judy would not be persuaded.

The governor's wife took the phone from her husband. "Are you going to need your container back?" she asked.

"They don't make that model anymore," said Judy.

"I understand completely," said the governor's wife.

The adviser was less forgiving. He leaked word of Judy's refusal to make chili for the governor to his favorite newspaper columnist, whose syndicated column about the incident was headlined "Chili Maker Chills Governor."

The story made Judy sound principled but in a slightly dotty way—like one of those people who refuses to sell his tumbledown tenement building to the developer who has offered him millions, forcing the developer to build his skyscraper around it.

The next day, Judy received an envelope by messenger from a famous morning T.V. news show hostess. Judy knew the woman slightly: she and Elaine had played with her as children, when their parents had all rented cottages at the same beach resort.

In her warm handwritten note, the hostess recalled that summer in far more detail than Judy could remember. Judy's memory of the hostess had mostly to do with her bathing suit (a two-piece that made Judy want to burn the one-piece her own mother had bought her) and watching her squirt lemon juice straight from the lemon onto her wavy long blonde hair.

The T.V. hostess wrote about how important Judy and Elaine's companionship had been for a lonely girl. "At the end of every glorious day on the beach, I dreaded going back to our bungalow—Daddy drunk again, Mother dropping her Southern belle act to shriek at him like a fishwife—and longed to be you or Elaine, heading home for supper with your families."

At the end of the note, almost as an afterthought, the hostess asked to interview Judy for her show. She would let Judy tell her story, and everyone could see what a lovely person she was.

Elaine cautioned against it. "I never liked her," she said. "She cheated at hearts."

Judy did not heed Elaine's advice. In the first place, Elaine had always been harshly critical of the T.V. hostess—she made sure to say, "She cheated at hearts," whenever the woman's name came up—and Judy sensed a strain of childhood jealousy in it.

More to the point, Judy was upset at the now-public perception of her as a character, an outspoken kooky lady. Mothers on the street steered their strollers in a swath around her, worried that she might frighten their children with a disagreeable word or look; college kids, who saw her as adorably truth telling, wore T-shirts that read "'Chili shouldn't have an agenda' —Chairman Judy."

So Judy went to the T.V. studio for her interview. Facing her across an enormous arrangement of chrysanthemums, the hostess reminisced about their summer together, remembering Judy as a person "of gravitas, even then," who represented "substance over style" (she had not forgotten Judy's bathing suit), while she herself, the product of an unhappy home life (she revealed no details, saving them for her memoirs), had been "hopelessly needy." Judy was not immune to flattery; she felt she was finally going to get a chance to tell her story.

"Knowing the stuff you're made of, then, I can't say it surprised me that you turned down the governor," said the hostess. "What I'm hearing is that it wasn't personal on your part—it's just that you prefer to make your chili for your friends."

"That's right," said Judy.

"So, Judy, do you think you might make some of your amazing chili for this old friend?"

"Well . . . sometime," said Judy, who was beginning to get a funny feeling.

"What if I had all the ingredients here, and I told you that nothing would give me greater pleasure than a bowl of your chili? Might you consider making me some right now?" asked the hostess.

"I guess I'd be uncomfortable not being in my own kit—" said Judy. She never watched morning television and had failed to notice what lay beyond the weather-map area in the studio.

"Let's go, girl!" said the hostess, who took any response to a request of hers, including "Drop dead," as a yes.

She grabbed Judy's arm and propelled her past the weather map to another set—a working kitchen. On the counter was every ingredient that could possibly be used to make chili.

"You do your magic," said the hostess, "and at the end of the show we'll bring on three surprise judges to sample the chili that brought a governor to his knees."

She smiled dazzlingly for the camera—then, as the program cut to a commercial, dashed off to call her Pilates instructor.

Judy considered leaving. But she had come to clear her name, not make more headlines. If she left, even those who had approved of her refusal to make chili for the governor would write her off as petulant, and no one likes to be written off as petulant by millions of people. She would make the damn chili, and that would be the end of it.

During the next hour, between interviewing a farmer who claimed to be able to forecast tornadoes with a pair of salad tongs and an eleven-year-old hacker who had sold the entire freshman class at Harvard the answers to the biochemistry final, the hostess checked in with Judy for on-air progress reports. Looking increasingly grim, Judy answered her questions in monosyllables.

Minutes before the end of the program, the three surprise judges came out and gathered around Judy at the stove. One was the show's jolly weatherman, one was the anchor of the network's evening newscast, and the third was a major movie star, who had agreed only because he was publicizing his dreadful new movie.

The hostess handed each of them a spoon. "Dig in!" she told them. Smiling, each of them put a big spoonful into his mouth.

Suddenly their eyes had the frantic look of those who know they are going to have to swallow something they would pay a thousand dollars to spit out.

A long silence followed. The weatherman and the movie star tried desperately to compose their thoughts, and their faces, in order to say something polite.

The anchor, a verbose but scrupulously honest person, spoke first. "Recently my wife and I attended a gala benefit dinner, and undercooked fiddlehead ferns were served. They tasted exactly like this concoction—bitter, oddly chalky. And, at the same time, loamy. Mulchy; of the earth."

His candor emboldened the others. "It tastes like dog food," said the weatherman, cracking up the crew by sticking out his tongue.

"It tastes like dog *excrement*," said the movie star, who then stalked off the set.

"Well, that was fun—*not*," said the hostess, who had a habit of throwing around stale catchphrases. Livid, she nonetheless smiled tightly. "I think it's safe to say that this particular batch of chili did have an agenda, and that agenda was, 'It's never too late to get even with someone who owned a bikini when you were stuck with a tank suit.'"

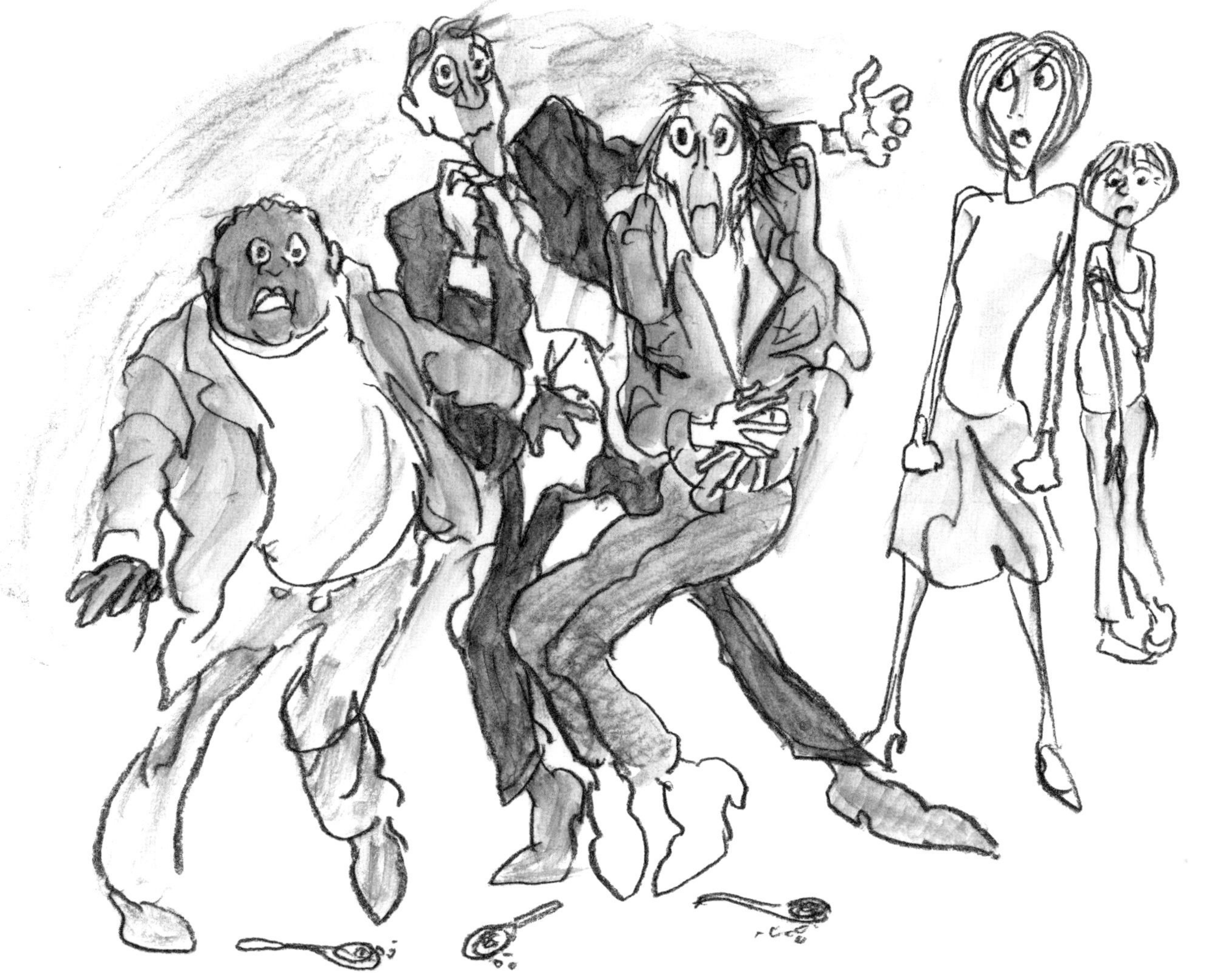

"I would never do that," said Judy.
"Tell me, Judy, is this really how you wanted to get famous?"
"I never wanted to get famous," said Judy. "And you cheated at hearts."

Judy became only more renowned after the interview—a crabby iconoclast who (as the T.V. hostess might have said if she hadn't vowed never to utter Judy's name again) told it like it was. Producers offered her her own reality show. "Love her or hate her—she's Judy!" was the opening tagline for the show that one producer suggested.

Elaine shook her head. "It's not even about the chili anymore."

"I don't ever want to talk about chili again," said Judy, who had put her chili pot away in a closet and had taken to spending too much time in her bathrobe.

Elaine told all their friends what Judy had said. And for the next three years, whenever they spoke to her, Judy's friends made their illnesses and disappointments and setbacks sound like minor nuisances, fearful that otherwise she might think they were chili mongering.

Then, early one Sunday morning, Elaine ran into Judy on the sidewalk. Judy was smiling and carrying a shopping bag; inside, Elaine could see, were two plastic containers filled with chili.

"My dental hygienist just had an oophorectomy," said Judy.
"I thought you said you never wanted to talk about chili again," said Elaine, feeling betrayed.

"I did. I didn't say I never wanted
to make it again," said Judy.

"Thank God," said Elaine,
throwing her arms around her
oldest friend.

"How's everything?" said Judy.

"So so," said Elaine. "Did I tell you about my rotator cuff?"

ABOUT THE AUTHORS

Jenny Allen writes magazine articles and essays and performs stand-up comedy.

Jules Feiffer is a cartoonist, playwright, and children's book author. He and his wife, Jenny Allen, live in New York with their two children.